OPTICAL ILLUSIONS

OVER **200** MIND BENDING IMAGES

Bath • New York • Singapore • Hong Kong • Cologne • Delhi
Melbourne • Amsterdam • Johannesburg • Shenzhen

First published by Parragon Books Ltd in 2013 and distributed by

Parragon Inc.
440 Park Avenue South, 13th Floor
New York, NY 10016
www.parragon.com

Copyright © Parragon Books Ltd
Text by Robert K. Ausbourne
Layout by Clarity Media

Cover design by Talking Design

ISBN 978-1-4723-2946-2

Printed in China

The Obama Illusion presents two faces of the president side by side. They both look fairly reasonable except that they are upside down. Turn the image right side up and get a big surprise! We are very good at recognizing faces, but recognizing individual facial features is a whole other kettle of fish.

Arrowheads

The Banded Arrowhead is a subtle form of the Fraser Spiral (see page 25). Reversed sets of arrowheads coerce an apparent unevenness to the horizontal rows.

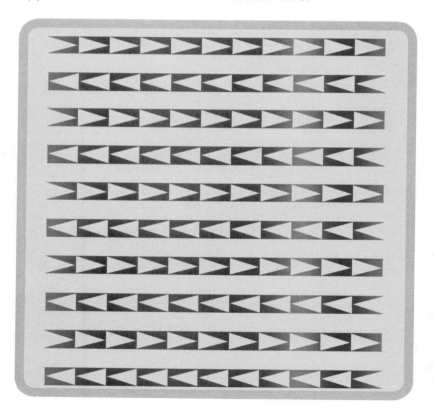

The Curved Cards is one of the oldest and best loved distortions. Except for color the two cards are identical. Whichever card happens to be on the left always appears larger. Knowing that we will compare the long gentle curve of one card to the short choppy curve of the other ensures the illusion. Cut these shapes out and place them back to back—the illusion will disappear. Use three or even four cards placed as shown. The illusion persists.

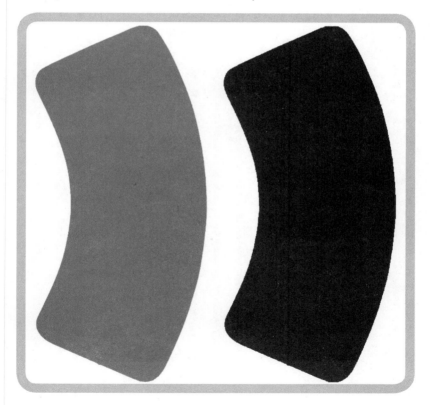

Bent Bars 1

The Herring, or sometimes Wundt, distortion is named after researchers who studied its effects more than 100 years ago. The background patterns cause the effect and the bars in the foreground are targets for distortion. The bars can seem to bend inward or outward at a whim of the background.

In this Herring variation the bars can seem to bend inward or outward at a whim of the background.

Bent Bars 3

In this Herring variation the bars appear to bend inward and outward in the same illusion.

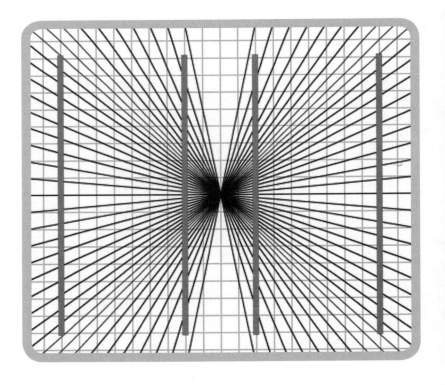

Busted Burst Circle

In this Herring variation the background is in the front and our view of the circle is subject to distortion.

Café Wall

The Café Wall distortion was discovered on a tiled storefront in Bristol, England. Even though they are uniform, these rows of tiles appear bent and uneven. The amount of offset in the black and white tiles, and the thickness of the grout lines, are influential in this distortion.

The Hidden Chain distortion happens when we try to track an oblique line behind an obstruction. The two parts of the continuous chain that we can see do not appear to meet behind the board, but they do.

Checkerboard Bulge

Checkerboard distortions are a rich source of illusory effects. The checkerboard design underneath is uniform and perfect. The distorted appearance is caused by objects placed in the foreground. A ruler will verify that all vertical and horizontal lines are actually straight.

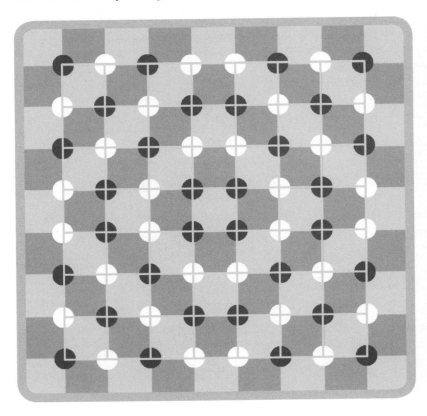

Checkerboard Stars

In this Checkerboard variation the distortion is generated by a simple pattern of tiny stars.

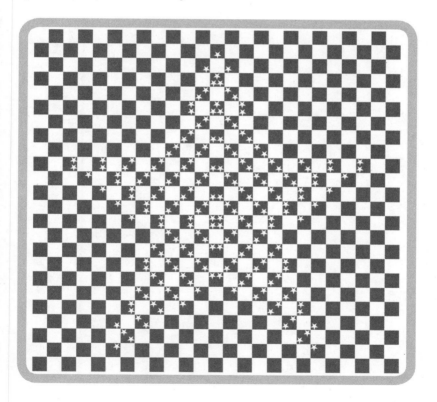

Checkerboard Squares

In this Checkerboard variation a wavy distortion is achieved by applying a pattern of tiny squares.

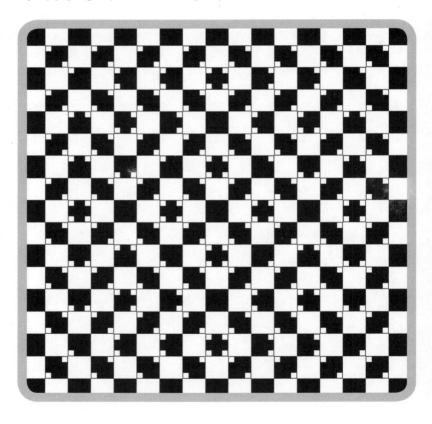

An extravagant formula of shapes gives this Checkerboard variation a three-dimensional rippling appearance.

Checkerboard Gears

Tiny gears replace the circles in this Checkerboard variation.

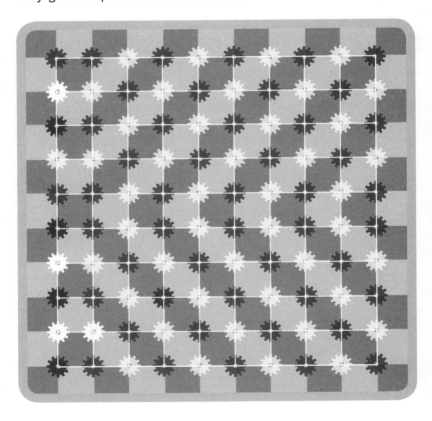

This is a Herring distortion mutation in which a circle is bent by a chevron-shaped background.

Bent Square Illusion

The circles in the background deceive us and cause the square in the center to appear bent when it is really straight. It may be that the concentric circles fool our brains into thinking that we must be moving. The square looks distorted and foreshortened as it might appear if we were moving.

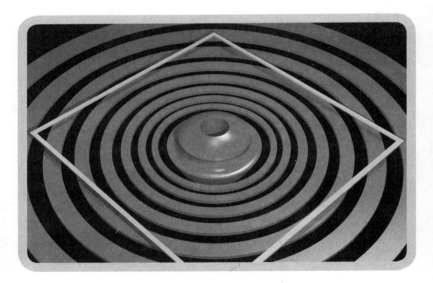

In this Herring variation the circles in the background cause the square in the foreground to appear to bow inward. The sparks are just for show.

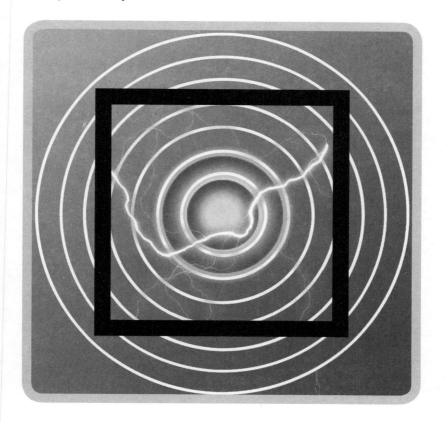

Crooked Dashes

All of the vertical lines and dashes shown in this variation of the Fraser Spiral (see page 25) are straight up and down.

The Crooked Gate distortion looks lopsided by using the same effects as the Fraser Spiral (see page 25).

Delboeuf Illusion

Which black circle is bigger in the Delboeuf Illusion? They are the same size. Both objects are influenced by their nearest neighbors, and we are presented with another distortion illusion.

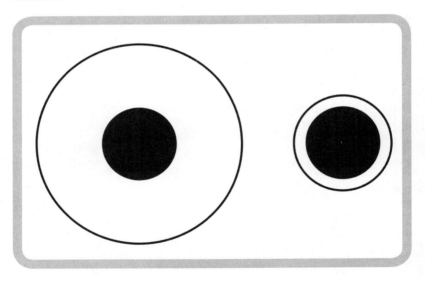

This is a three-dimensional version of the classic Titchener Illusion. Which of the central balls is larger? Both are the same size.

Fraser Illusion Rope

This variation of the Fraser Spiral, or Braided Rope effect
(see opposite page), makes these horizontal rows of
diamond shapes appear crooked.

Here is the classic Fraser Spiral distortion illusion. The Spiral is not really a spiral. It is actually a series of concentric circles. The twisted ropy, "braided" design of the circles makes us think we see a spiraling pattern.

Here is the classic Herring distortion illusion shown in reverse, where the horizontal lines appear to be bent inward.

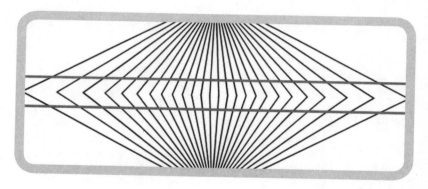

The Horizon illusion is one of perspective. The two images shown side by side are identical, yet they give the impression of being radically different in perspective. The distortion is caused by the fact that the images are touching and because the brain wants to assume they are a single image. If this is so, then all objects must point toward a single vanishing point on the horizon. However, they don't, and we perceive a distortion.

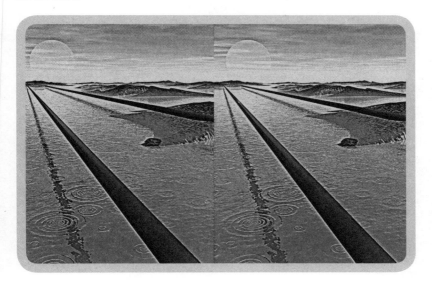

Lincoln's Hat

Here is the classic Lincoln's Hat illusion. The president's stovepipe hat is exactly as high as its brim is wide. The rule: A vertical line that intersects a horizontal line will always appear longer.

In this Lincoln's Hat variation (see opposite page), the distance between dot one on the left in the horizontal row and the dot overhead is the same as the distance between dot one and dot three on the right in the horizontal row. The rule: A vertical line that intersects a horizontal line will always appear longer in comparison.

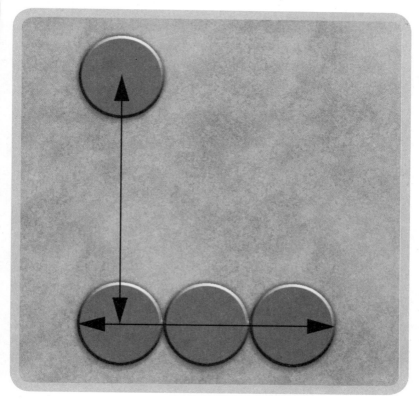

The letters that make up the word "LIFE" in this variation of the Fraser Spiral (see page 25) are not crooked; they just look that way. Grab a ruler and prove it to yourself.

The Mystic Wheel's spokes are all flat, yet we cannot help but perceive the wheel as three-dimensional. The ripples in the spokes become either humps or hollows. Any ripple will appear hollow on one side of the design and humped on the other. If you turn the design upside down, the humps and hollows will remain the same because we assume the light source hasn't changed.

Poggendorf Illusion

This is the classic Poggendorf Illusion. Which of the black lines is continuous from top to bottom? A ruler will prove that it is the lowest line on the right that is connected to the top line segment. If the lines were all horizontal or vertical, we would have no trouble tracking them behind the obstruction. However, oblique lines give us a little distortional trouble.

A classic distortion called the Ponzo Illusion after a researcher, this distortion is caused by an "assumed" perspective. We assume that the peaked line segment must act similar to a railroad track; it should get smaller in the distance. The horizontal lines are the same length, but the top one appears longer because we assume it must be farther away on the tracks.

Pyramid Dots

Here is a plan view of the classic Pyramid distortion illusion. Which of the vertical dots most closely marks the vertical center of the triangle? If you think it is number three, guess again. Dot number two most closely marks the center.

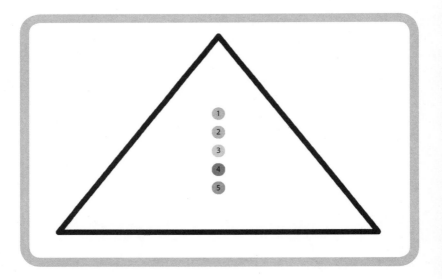

This illusion illustrates the power and treachery of images. There is no real perspective here; it's just ink on a page. Each dot merely gets skinnier as they progress across the image. Yet our brains are happy to assume that there is real depth and a gentle curve.

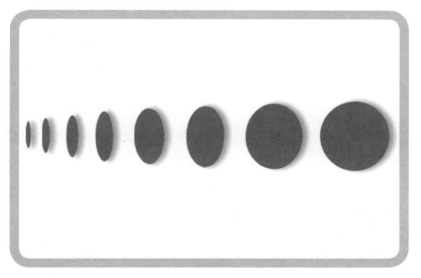

Days Sine Illusion

In this design of a mirrored sine wave the vertical dashes are all identical. They only appear to be shorter or longer according to their position within the wave.

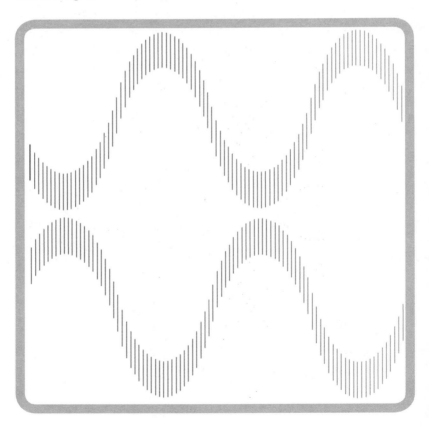

In this variation of the Horizon distortion illusion (see page 27), we are presented with two views of a building. The images are identical, yet one building looks like it is leaning at a different angle. We are assuming that the two images are one, and, therefore, both buildings should point at the same place in the sky.

Zöllner Illusion

In the classic Zöllner, or sometimes Herringbone Illusion, reversed herringbone patterns on the parallel lines distort our perception and to us the lines look crooked.

This variation of the Zöllner Illusion (see opposite page) uses reversed segments of chains to accomplish the distortion of the horizontal symmetry.

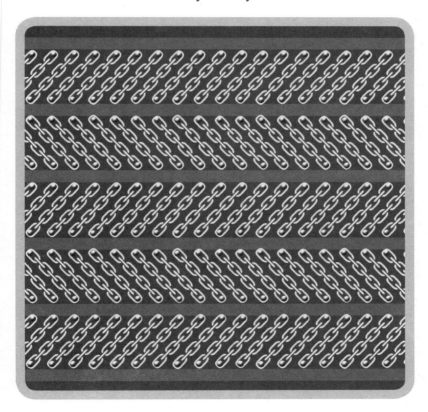

Palm Tree

The Palm Tree distortion is a variation of the Zöllner Illusion (see page 38). Here, a herringbone pattern of lines makes the trees appear to lean in different directions.

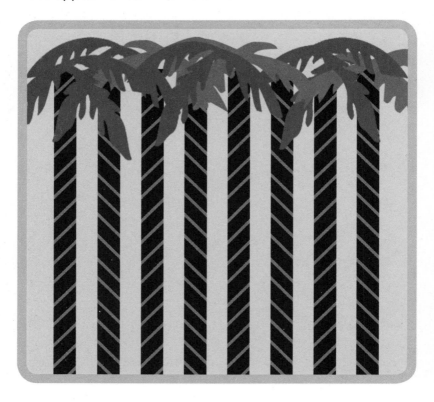

This variation of the Zöllner Illusion (see page 38) is self-explanatory.

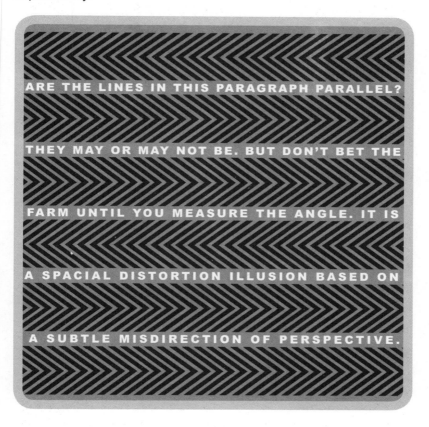

ARE THE LINES IN THIS PARAGRAPH PARALLEL?

THEY MAY OR MAY NOT BE. BUT DON'T BET THE

FARM UNTIL YOU MEASURE THE ANGLE. IT IS

A SPACIAL DISTORTION ILLUSION BASED ON

A SUBTLE MISDIRECTION OF PERSPECTIVE.

Two Bottles And One Glass

Two aspects share the same contours in this figure;
one wine glass and two bottles.

Two Glasses And One Bottle

What do you see here? In this elegant ambiguity there are two glasses and one bottle—with a cork.

The Missing Corner Illusion has three aspects: 1) a cube with a missing corner in the front; 2) a hollow room with two walls and a floor, with a small cube sitting in the back corner; and 3) a large cube with a small cube floating separately in front. Note: Build a model of this illusion—rotate the model in your hand and watch as the little cube in aspect (3) rotates backward!

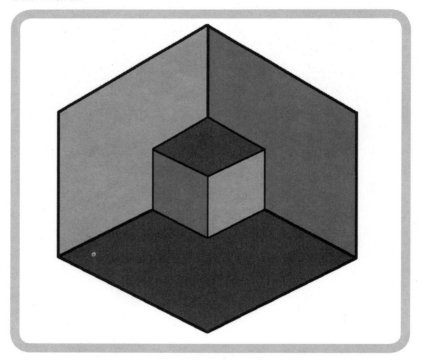

This patterned rendering of the Missing Corner Illusion (see opposite page) may help us obtain closure with all three aspects.

Illustration by Arthur Azevedo

This three-dimensional figure can be seen as three blocks with a cross-shaped piece missing from the front, or the cross shape can be seen as floating in front of the blocks.

The Reversible Stairs is another classic. In this view the steps have gray tops and a black background. Flip the image over and the steps now have gray fronts and a white background.

Ambiguous Pillars

In *Piliers de l'ambiguïté*, or the Ambiguous Pillars, there is something about these columns that makes them ambiguous. If you look closely at the spaces between the columns, you will find several figures in profile.

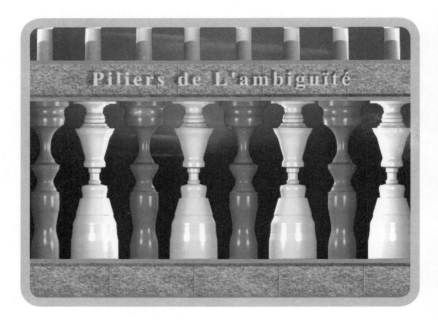

Candle And Lovers Illusion

The Candle and Lovers Illusion is a crafty ambiguity.
Can you avoid figure/ground confusion and find both the
lovers and the candle? Hint: The candle is in the foreground,
and the lovers are part of the background.

Baby Illusion

This drawing shows a young couple daydreaming beside a lake. Can you find what they are dreaming about? A baby maybe?

Several scientists were studying this photo of a distant planet. They were arguing about what it could be. Some were sure it was a natural feature, while others leaned toward a lava bulge getting ready to erupt. They argued for hours until a worker walked by and innocently turned the picture around. Turn the picture around yourself and see what the humbled scientists saw.

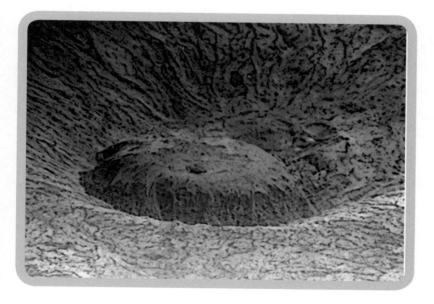

The Book Illusion can be seen as open and facing you; or open and facing away from you. Can you obtain closure with both aspects?

Buffalo Bill's Wild West

This old poster from Buffalo Bill's Wild West Show is a drawing of Buffalo Bill made entirely of related objects. How many can you find?

Cats In A Pattern

This tessellated pattern has gray cats facing to the right.
Can you find the black cats? Hint: Flip the image over.

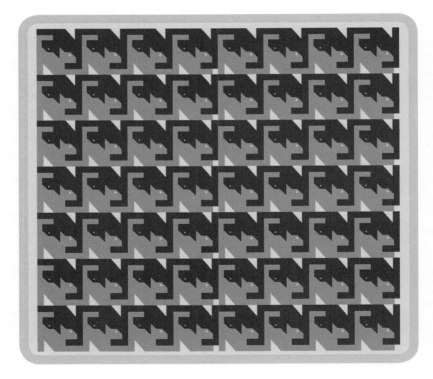

Do you see a tunnel in this geometric pattern? Do you see a cone shape?

Field Of Cubes

In this Field of Cubes, do you see the cubes with dark bottoms? Or with dark tops? A canny viewer in complete closure will see both.

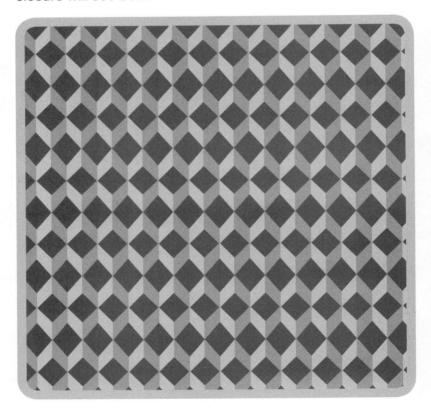

Do you see dimples in the center and bumps all around in the Bumpy Plate Illusion? Can you imagine that the light comes from below and see bumps in the center and dimples all around?

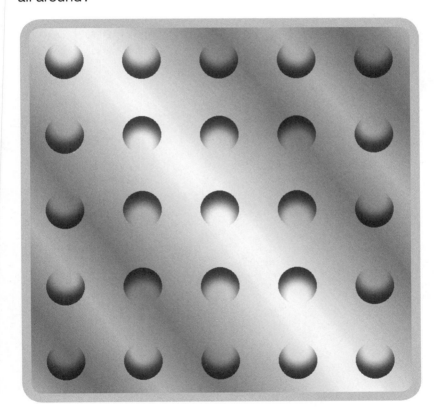

Cup Profile

This *objet d'art* from an illustrated catalog comes complete with two open-mouthed profiles. Can you find them?

The Telephone Illusion is so old that this instrument wouldn't work for texting. But then again, my smart phone doesn't have profiles of two cute dogs built into the design.

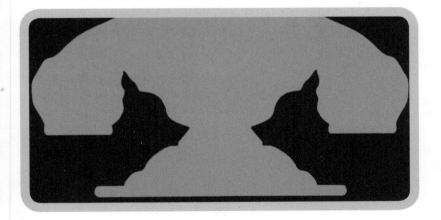

The Eight Illusion shows the figure 8 cutout of wood sitting in a large circle, which is also cut out of wood. Rotate the image 180 degrees. The background is now solid wood, and the figure 8 is part of the background!

Illustration by Arthur Azevedo

Can you find a Native American Chief and an Eskimo in this drawing?

Face Or Barbell?

This illusion is either a toothy, bearded guy with dark glasses, or a strongman lifting a barbell.

Do you see the falcon bird design in this illusion,
or the face of Professor Falcon?

Smiling Man Or Mouse?

This illusion is simply ambiguous. Do you see a whiskered mouse, or a smiling man?

Is this a slipper, or a man with dark hair and glasses?

Father And Son

In the Father and Son illusion, can you find them both?
Hint: the old guy's prominent nose has a bump, which is very
close to the son's Roman nose.

The Third Generation Illusion contains a portrayal of the daughter, the mother, and the grandfather. Can you find all three? Hint: The mother needs the daughters choker, the grandfather does not. Good luck!

Tropical Fish Or Owl?

This charming painting of two tropical fish kissing is hiding an owl in plain sight. Can you find the hooter?
Hint: The owl takes an eye from each.

The Necker Cube is a famous wire-framed rectangle that can change spatial geometry in a twinkle as you watch. The small end in front can face forward or backward, but the top is always the top. The fish looks like it is inside, and then sometimes outside the "tank."

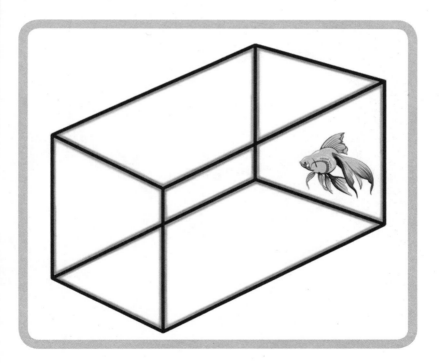

This pen and ink drawing can be seen as either a woman wrapped in a blanket, or the clenched fist of someone that needs a manicure.

Contrasting hues and shades on the Folded Star illusion give it a three-dimensional look, which causes it to appear folded in various directions.

Girl And Mother

This richly illustrated example of the multiple-face type
illusion is so old that it may be one of the first of its kind. The
young girl faces away in profile; the old hag faces left with
a choker for a mouth. The choker (mouth) element appears
omnipresent in all variations.

This Figure/Ground Illusion also has two profiles. The figure of the vase is in the foreground; the profiles belong, for the most part, to the background—hence, figure/ground illusion.

Goose Illusion

Is this a drawing of a goose flying west, or a hawk flying east? Okay, the direction doesn't matter.

Is this a drawing of the cutest little Mouse, or the cutest little Hippo?

Today And Tomorrow

Today and Tomorrow is an allegory/skull theme from long ago. Here, we see the happy couple celebrating as a skulking skull lurks in the background.

H. M. Rose, circa 1900

The outline of Idaho has a locally famous ambiguous illusion along its state border. Can you find the old potato farmer? Of course, Montana, the next state over, must have the same illusion in reverse, right? Can you find the old sheep herder?

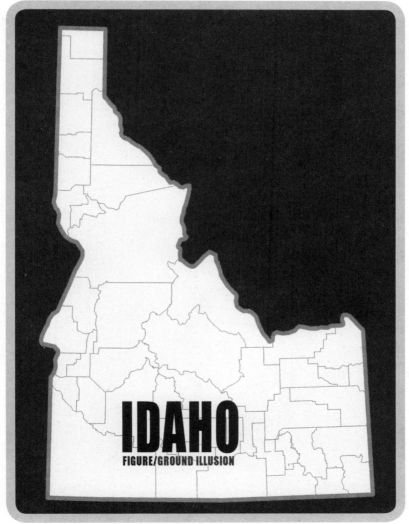

IDAHO
FIGURE/GROUND ILLUSION

Christ's Eyes

This painting of Christ from around the early twentieth century has become iconic because of the eyes. If you stare at them long enough, they seem to open and close.

Gabriel Max, *Veronica's Handkerchief*, 1915

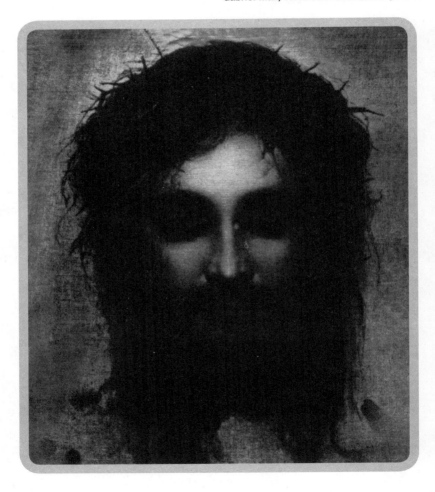

This design for an iron hitching post has Abraham Lincoln's face all over it—literally. The president's profile, with beard and famous hat, are wrapped continuously around the post. It doesn't matter how you view it, there are always two profiles to see.

Lovers And Skull

A lurking skull is featured in yet another allegorical print. This time the skull is bound by bowers of greenery and some wine.

Marble Winged Butterflies

The Marble Winged Butterfly is one of the most beautiful denizens …wait, make those two Marble Winged Butterflies, mating.

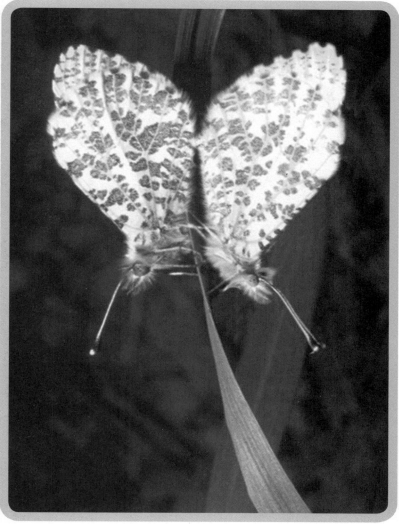

Mermaid Illusion

The Mermaid Illusion shows a posing mermaid and a crone, which share the same space in this drawing.

Females And Hooded Nuns

Within the foreground color (black) of this design there is
a row of female forms, while in the background color (white)
there is a gang of hooded nuns.

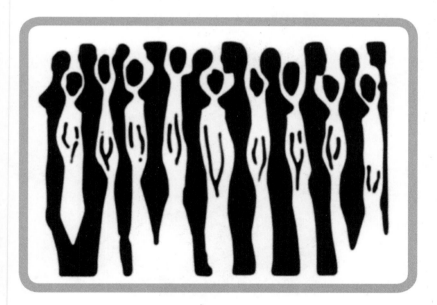

The saxophone player is hiding a woman's face. Can you find her?

The elephant looks like an elephant; where is the seashell?

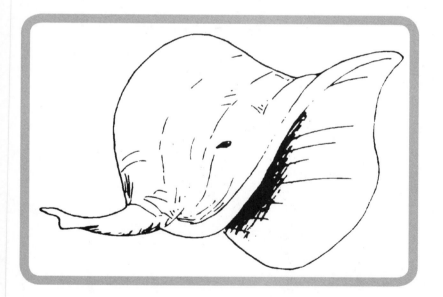

Cork Screw Illusion

The Cork Screw Illusion is also an Indian basket with a rearing cobra snake.

The Swan Illusion is also the Squirrel Illusion.
Can you spot both aspects?

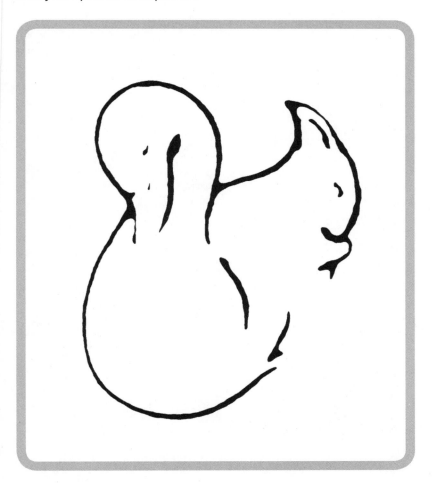

Society: A Portrait

This is an example from the pen of George Wotherspoon, called Society: A Portrait. It shows a dandy out on the town with his consorts. Gosh, this guy really looks like an ass!

George Wotherspoon, circa 1900

The Eagle Of The Republic

On this Civil war era trading card, the card reads, "The Eagle of the Republic: what do you see in this picture?"

L. Prang & Co., Country Clerks Office of the District Court of Mass., 1865

Answer: The design contains the hidden faces of Jefferson Davis, George Washington, and Abraham Lincoln.

89

With a written form as robust as the English language, there are bound to be ambiguities. In this figure the letter "A" could easily stand for the letter "H."

THE CHT

An old postcard illustration called, "The Tie That Binds" blends a woman's figure with a necktie to create ambiguity.

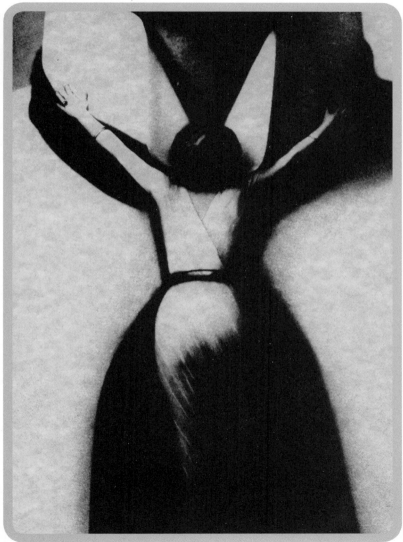

How many tools can you identify in the Tool Set Illusion?

Answer: Don't forget figure/ground confusion, and count tools in the background as well!

Turkey And Eskimo Illusion

Oh no! Not another Turkey–Eskimo Illusion!

This whimsical old sketch is both an island and a reclining bearded man.

Wenzel Hollar, circa fifteenth century

Young And Old Woman

The earliest known version of the Young–Old Woman Illusion and probably the original, this delightfully ambiguous figure is called "My Wife and My Mother-in-Law."

Illustrated by W. E. Hill, from *Puck* magazine, 1915

Curious Optical Illusion

Cartoonists are wonderful sources of ambiguity. The caption of the cartoon reads; "A curious optical illusion caused by a lady forgetting the number of her bathing machine."

Illustrated by William Heath Robinson

A photo taken in 1981 during a test flight of a U.S. fighter jet has an amazing ambiguity. The cast shadow below the jet makes it look like it is flying low to the ground, and yet the surrounding terrain features indicate that the fighter must be huge—way out of scale. What is going on? Hint: The cast shadow is really a large lake far below the jet.

Woman Of The World

What is the Woman of the World Illusion? Where is the ambiguity? Hint: The title, plus what is round and has continents?

Hidden among the major continents and oceans is the outline of a woman's head.

What do these blobs of ink mean? Hint: Think; Mercator Projection, or rotate the image?

Can you see the eagle in the east rim of the Grand Canyon?

A face staring upward to the sky in Bandon, Oregon. See how many faces you can recognize on the subsequent pages.

59 rue de Rivoli, Paris, France

This Samurai Crab is shown sporting a believable mask of an ancient Japanese warrior. The story has it that this species of crab only looked a little like a Japanese warrior in the beginning. Centuries of fishermen taking the crabs, and honorably releasing those crabs that looked most like samurai, and which lived to reproduce, have fostered the contemporary picture-perfect Samurai Crab. Could this be a case of unnatural selection?

Rijksmuseum van Natuurlijke Historie, Leiden, the Netherlands

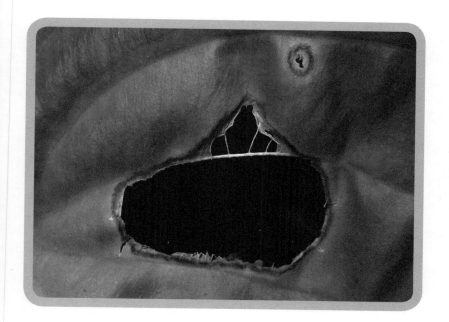

"Those are not the Droids you want." This is a camera used for videoconferencing.

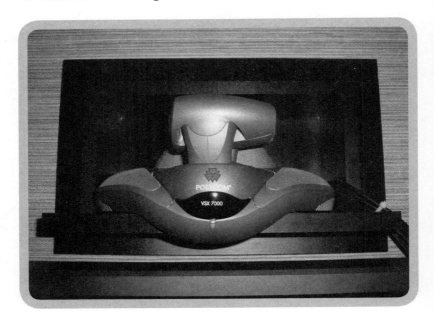

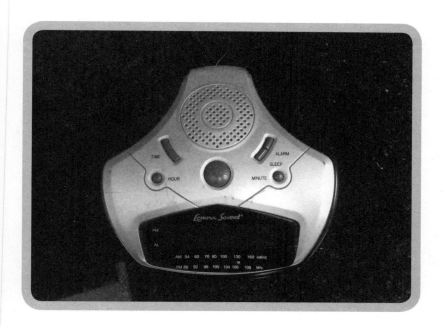

Medicine Lodge State Park.

Ship Rock in the Navaho Indian Nation, near the town of Shiprock, New Mexico.

Arcimboldo Vegetables

See how many "topsy-turvy illusions" you can solve on the
subsequent pages by simply turning them upside down.
Turn this image upside down to see why fans refer to
Giuseppe Arcimboldo lovingly as "Old Fruit Face."

Giuseppe Arcimboldo, *Man in the Fruit Bowl*

Help this street-hardened detective "Find the Killer."

A frog is looking for tasty flies, and hopes a nearby horse has brought some. Can you find the horse?

Old Dobbins is waiting patiently for his owner.
Can you help find him?

Angry Fellow

An old Japanese print shows an angry fellow.
Can you cheer him up?

This old gentleman looks upon life with disappointment and regret. Can you change his disposition?

This British bulldog is from a popular series of topsy-turvies published during World War I. Reverse the image to see the German Kaiser "on the run."

Here, the Kaiser is looking behind with a worried look, while Lord Kitchener is winking and smiling.

Missing Monk

A monk has come to the priory seeking help.
Can you help find his missing twin?

Cartoonist Peter Newell was very popular for his Topsy-Turvy books and cartoons. For a time, the entire nation was "flipping" over his work.

Peter Newell, *Topsys and Turvys, Topsys and Turvys Number 2,* 1893

A hermit with a long red beard dwelt in a lonely place.

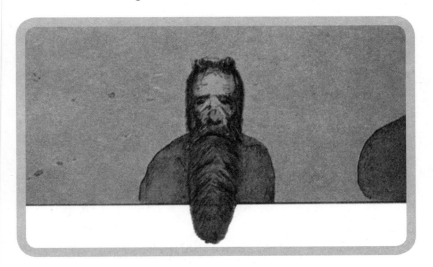

The squirrel gazed with wonder upon his gloomy face

This reversible is often found with the caption, "Before 8 beers, and after."

Cheerful man becomes thoughtful sage.

Faces, faces. Who's got more faces?

More faces?

Celebrities have always been a favorite theme for afterimage illusions. The trick is to stare at this and develop an afterimage and identify the famous person. Who is this famous pilot?

Answer: Charles Lindbergh

This famous person is known by many.

Answer: Jesus of Nazareth

Identify this famous revolutionary figure in afterimage.

Who is this "lighter-than-air" commander?

Can you identify this famous actress?

Answer: Greta Garbo

Can you identify this well-loved actress?

Can you name this U.S. president?

Answer: Thomas Jefferson

He was a famous leader during World War I. Can you name him?

Can you name this self-taught, rail-splitting U.S. president?

This is not a person but a famous painting. Can you name it?

Good-bye Norma Jean. Can you name this actress?

Answer: Marilyn Monroe

This U.S. president was sometimes called "Tricky Dickie". Can you name him?

Particles

As you stare at this design, ghostly afterimage "particles" will begin to swirl and race around the circles.

Give this image a fixed stare for a few seconds and then move your eyes slightly. White dots will appear among the black.

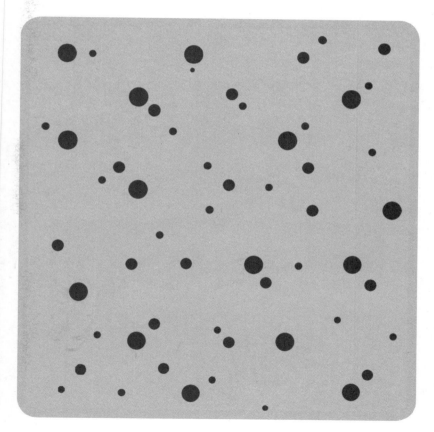

Burning Fuse Illusion

The center of the Burning Fuse Illusion appears zapped in white heat. The center is not brighter, it is an illusion caused by the dark cross ramping down to meet in the center. You might also see a darker "halo" around the center. This is dark color "bleeding" into open areas from the cross.

Illustration by Arthur Azevedo

In this variation of the Burning Fuse illusion, the center of the crossbeams is not really brighter than the white of the page. It only looks so—in contrast.

Circle Illusion

This star shape has so many points that they melt into a mist. There is also a curious moiré pattern that forms within the shape.

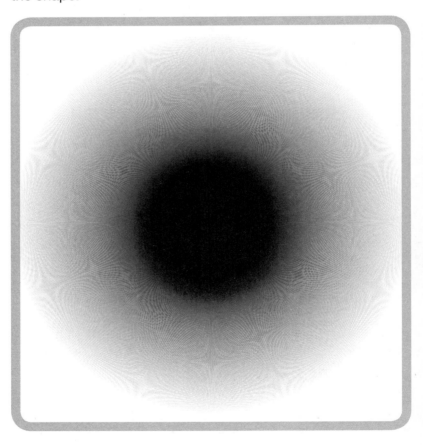

Here is another geometric pattern with a contrast illusion. The white color in the center is not brighter than any other white color nearby.

Contrasting Dots

Here is an elegant example of a contrast illusion.
The gray dots are identical in color and hue.

The Cornsweet Illusion is an excellent example of color bleeding. Both halves of the figure are identical in color and hue. The left appears darker because color is bleeding over the left-hand side from just the tiny shadow line down the center. Cover the tiny shadow line with your finger, pencil, or strip of paper and you will see that the areas on either side of the center are identical.

Flashing Dots Illusion

The Flashing Dots Illusion is more than just an afterimage illusion; it's also a contrast illusion. The white dots look brighter because they each have a huge amount of black nearby. This enhances the afterimage illusion. The dots will flash on and off as you gaze at the figure.

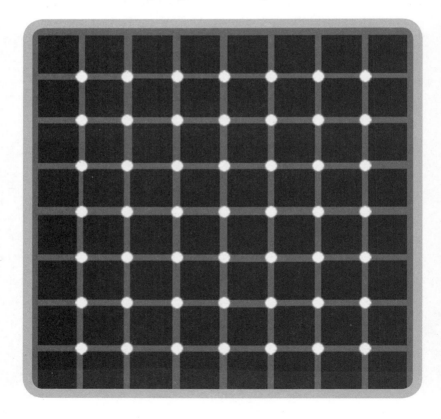

The Doughnuts on a Tablecloth is an experiment in contrast. The doughnuts are all the same; the idea is to see how the random shades of gray in the background affect how they appear.

Here is another exploration of the Doughnuts on a Tablecloth illusion.

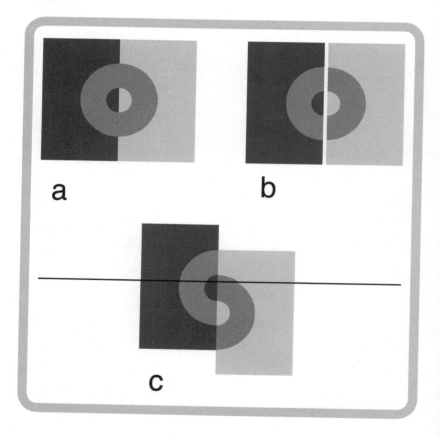

Contrasting Dashes

The columns and rows of black and white dashes create contrast havoc on the neutral gray background in this figure.

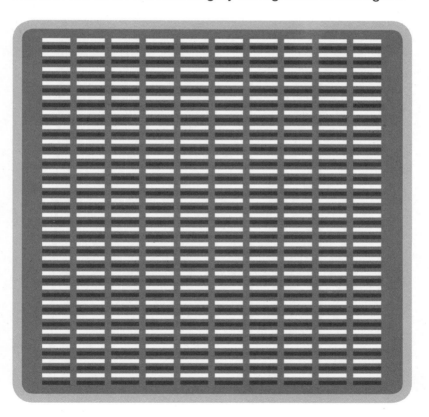

Burning Fuse Variation 1

This variation of the Burning Fuse Illusion (see page 146) creates the same effect in a grid pattern.

Illustration by Arthur Azevedo

Here is another variation of the Burning Fuse Effect (see page 146).

Illustration by Arthur Azevedo

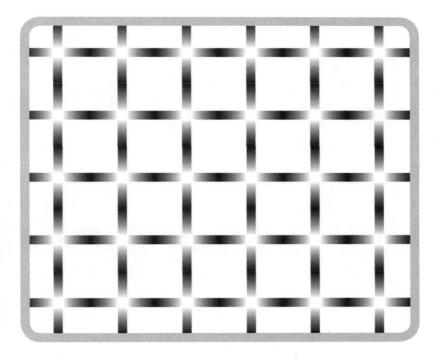

Gray Hearts

This design for a greeting card shows the effects of contrast on identical hearts within different background hues.

This example presents a little powerhouse of contrast. The chunky bit of checkerboard is uniform, with alternating squares of light and dark hues. A gray column casts a shadow across the board. Compare square (A) with square (B). Yes, they're the same hue! The squares around (B) are darker because they are in shadow—they make (B) look lighter. Square (A) is mostly surrounded by light squares— these squares make (A) look darker. The two contrast illusions combined to create a single fantasy in contrast.

Original design: R. Beau Lotto

McCourt Effect

This figure is an artful variation on background influence. The bar going across is all one single hue of gray.

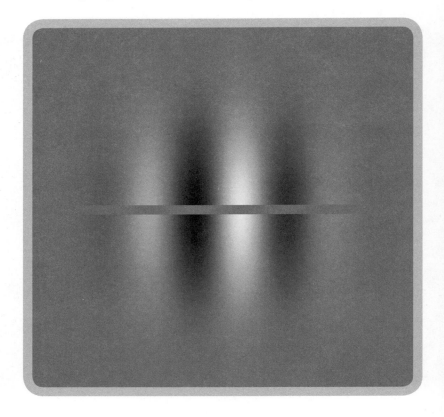

The so-called Ouchi Illusion demonstrates a dazzling contrast effect. As you stare at the figure, the background pattern will tend to separate and shimmer beneath the circle in the foreground.

Here is another version of the Ouchi Illusion (see page 161) with similar effects.

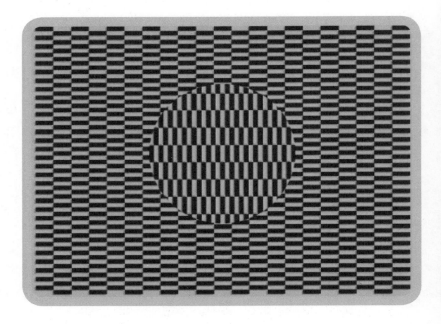

In the Pin-stripe Illusion, the gray hue is the same throughout the figure. Black influences the inner square and white rules the large square.

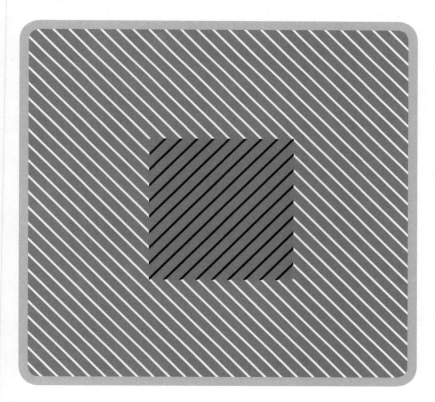

Each pair of dashes is identical in hue. Each background regulates a dashed pair's appearance with a contrast illusion.

The Ten Percent Illusion goes from 100 percent white to 100 percent black in ten steps. The center bar is 50 percent black throughout.

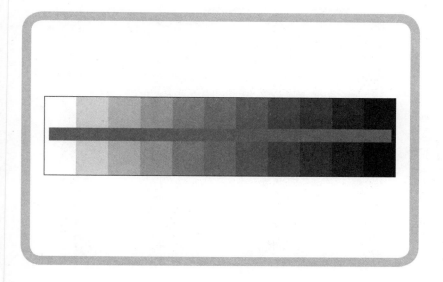

Three Drums

The white tape holding these drums together is all one hue.

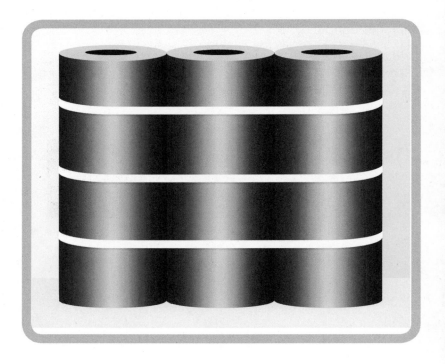

Because of contrast it is easy to imagine that the black rectangle is behind a translucent gray square. Or it's just three shapes. Or the black square is magnifying the gray square underneath. Or...

The Impossible Triangle, or Triad or sometimes the Tri-bar illusion, is the simplest most elegant impossible object anyone has ever designed. Oscar Reutersvärd created the world's first triad design. Roger Penrose, cofounder of the Big Bang Theory, called the triad design, "Impossibility in its purest form."

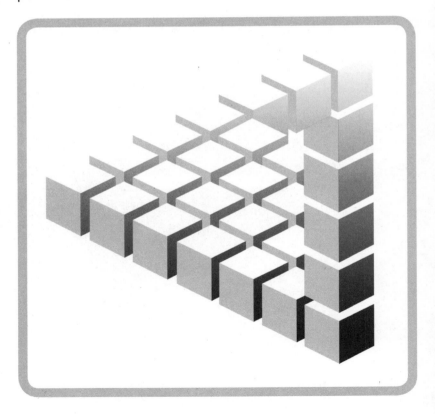

This variation of the impossible Triangle design is made from identical blocks. There are two sides with seven blocks and one side with six blocks. Hey! That's impossible.

An impossible square design set in a goopy alien landscape.

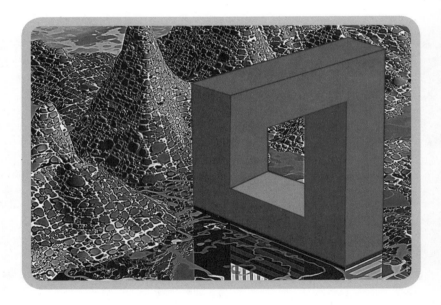

In the Bent Pencil Illusion, unless the pencil is rubberized, it cannot bend this way.

Bent Rectangle On A Table

Rigid rectangles on the table cannot bend this way, and this one can't either. It just looks that way. It's impossible.

Three rugged and rigid rings can certainly link up in this way, but they can't lie flat like this. It's impossible.

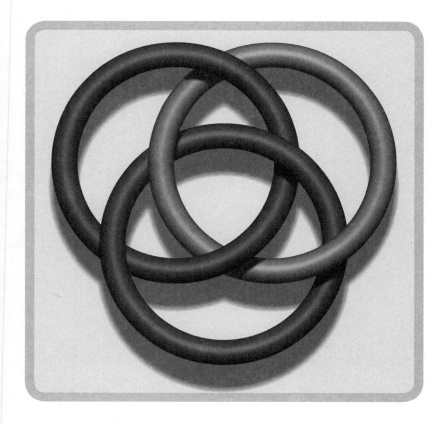

This schematic contains three impossible hexnuts, one impossible square, and a threaded Devil's Fork (see page 178). Give this drawing to your technical department; drive 'em nuts.

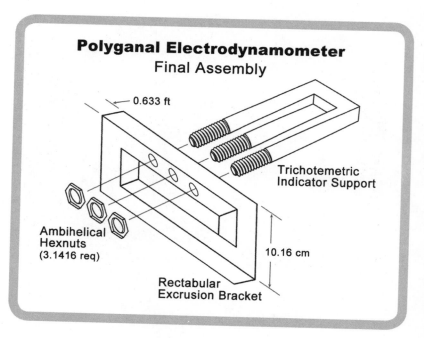

Polyganal Electrodynamometer
Final Assembly

0.633 ft

Trichotemetric
Indicator Support

Ambihelical
Hexnuts
(3.1416 req)

10.16 cm

Rectabular
Excrusion Bracket

Impossible Chessboard

Both ends of the board seem to face forward and the chess pieces are hanging every which way; this game is going to last impossibly long.

Corporate Ladder Illusion

No matter how fast and how far you climb, you will never get anywhere on this stairway. The staircase goes endless up or endlessly down.

A resort offers this new water sports feature, but people are complaining. The stairs don't go anywhere—except to the same level!

Classic Devil's Fork

In the Classic Devil's Fork, or Trident Illusion, it starts out a solid rectangle and ends up a threaded round fork.

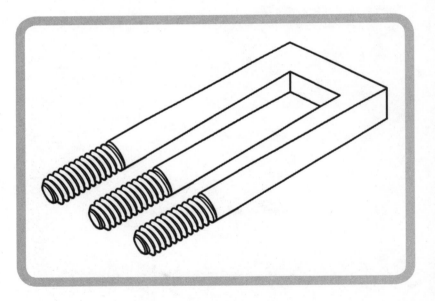

A variation of the Devil's Fork design (see opposite page).

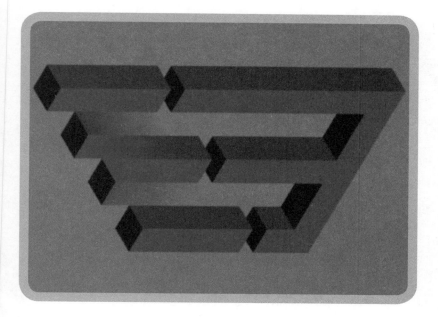

False Stairs

Faux Escalier, or False Stairs, is an illustrated impossible stair design.

These three gears cannot work. Places where the gears mesh are hopelessly twisted. The gears "share" contours and could not exist alone. They could not turn either.

This 18th century drawing by artist William Hogarth has many things wrong with it. How many can you find?

In this homage to Sandro Del-Prête, the wheel can never do any work.

Original design by **Sandro Del-Prête**, *Quadrature of the Wheel*

Hollow Steps Illusion

These steps are hollow on one side and normal on the other.
It's impossible!

These three blocks cannot fit together as they are pictured. What's wrong?

Impossible Triangle Sculpture

This outdoor sculpture looks impossible from one single viewing angle. If you look at it from any other angle, it looks like three arms going off in different directions. Within this narrow parameter impossible objects can exist!

East Perth, Western Australia

This ticket booth is impossible. If you see one of these at the carnival, run back to your spaceship—you are not on planet earth!

Impossible Form

This impossible form looks okay until ... you get to the vertical bar on the front.

A salute to Oscar Reutersvärd, creator of the world's first impossible triangle design in 1934.

Original design by Oscar Reutersvärd, *Opus 1,* 1934

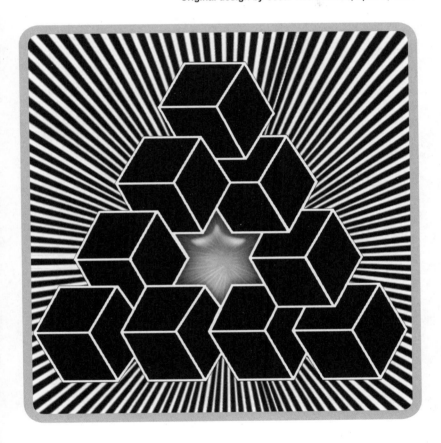

Pencils can intertwine like this, but not as shown. It's impossible.

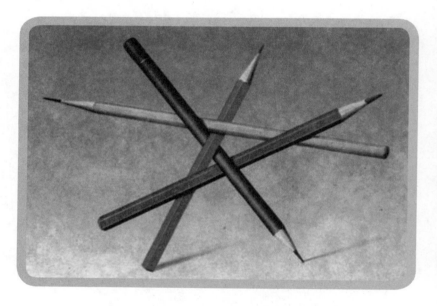

These pairs of pizza slices cannot fit together in this way. Why?

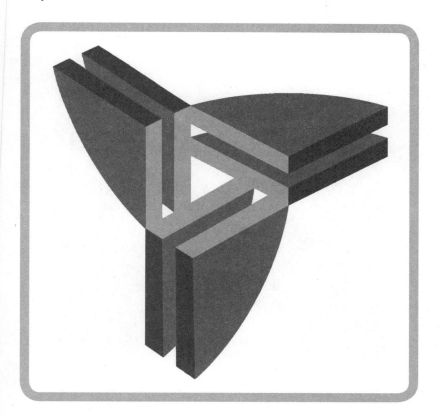

Impossible Wood Stack

Not many people would stack wood as shown here.

A cube may be dissected in this way, but it would never look like this.

This photograph has been rigged to remove some of the details and all of the color except black and white. Can you spot all six zebras in the photo? If you were a hungry lion, this is pretty close to what you would see … better lie low and wait for something to move.

This photograph from World War I shows the troopship
Prince of Wales fully camouflaged in razzle dazzle paint.
Camouflage patterns weren't meant to hide a ship, but rather
to confuse an enemy observer. An observer, after spotting
the ship, must quickly report her exact position, course and
speed. (This was before radar.) A camouflaged ship matches
the color of the sky and sports large dark and confusing
shapes. Lacking visual clues, the observer cannot easily
tell if the ship is coming toward him or going away. By the
time he figures it out, the Prince of Wales could be over the
horizon—safely beyond range.

What is hidden in this camouflaged pattern?

Can you find a spotted white cat in this wintry scene?

What do you see here?

Answer:

198

Sometimes the best camouflage is to clam up, and act like you belong. Can you spot the quarry?

Grasshopper

"Become the leaf Grasshopper." Can you spot the camouflaged bug?

This leaf-shaped moth is well suited to its environment.

This old cartoon's caption reads, "Find the Bridegroom."
Does he really exist? Can you find him?

Here is an anamorphic illusion that is also an advertising card for a Victorian garment retailer. The way to reveal the illusion is to stare at the vertical line in the center while slowly drawing the image closer to your eyes. The two halves will merge in the mind's eye and the lady will model the merchandise.

THE JOHN BRESSMER CO.
DRY GOODS, CARPETS, ETC.
Springfield, Ill.

Stereoscopic Cat

Stare at the center of this image and gently cross your eyes until the two images merge to complete the design.

Find the hidden face in this drawing.

Answer: Rotate the image 90 degrees counterclockwise. The face is in the center of the image.

205

Anamorphic Message 1

This graphic design hides a message that is also a palindrome. A palindrome is a special kind of sentence that reads the same forward and backward. To reveal the message, you must view the image in the correct way. Try rotating the image clockwise 90 degrees then tilt the top of the image away from you drastically.

Answer: Are we not drawn onward, we few, drawn onward to new era?

This anamorphic message is a very simple, single word. Tilt the top of the image away from you until you can read the message.

Niagara

Tilt the top of the image away from you until the message becomes readable. The message is also a palindrome, a word or phrase that reads the same forward and backward.

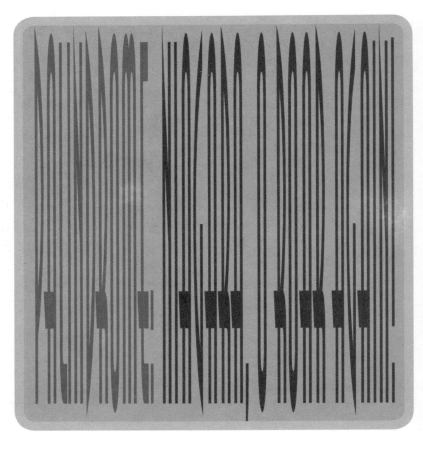

Answer: PALINDROME: NIAGRA, O ROAR AGAIN.

Anamorphic Palindrome

Here is another anamorphic puzzle that is also two palindromes (see opposite page). Tilt the top of the image away from you to reveal the message.

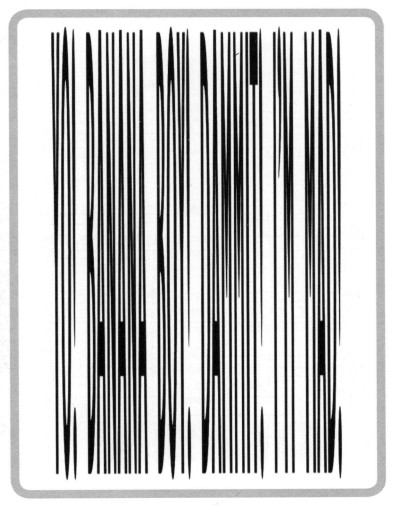

Christmas Card

This design for a Christmas card has two hidden greetings. Can you decipher them both?

Answers: MERRY CHRISTMAS! and HAVE A HAPPY NEW YEAR!

This old Valentine's Day card has an anamorphic message. Can you decipher Cupid's message?

When should a pretty girl be hugged? Can you work out the answer in this anamorphic changeling?

Answer: WHEN DANGEROUS CIRCUMSTANCES REQUIRE HER TO BE "ARMED."

Why are women so wicked? Solve the anamorphic puzzle to find the answer.

Answer: BECAUSE THEY STEEL THEIR CORSETS, CRIB THEIR BABIES, AND HOOK ONE ANOTHER'S DRESSES.

213

Big Wave

This figure generates a rippling effect. Keep your eyes moving! Did you notice that the little squares have black and white edges? These edges are powering the effect. The direction of apparent movement is based on which side is white or black.

From original designs by Akiyoshi Kitaoka

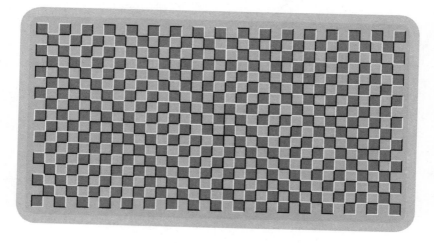

This high-tech drawing may appear to bulge as you gaze into its metallic countenance.

Curtain

This variation ripples back and forth in long rows. Do white edges on the oval shapes point in the direction of movement? What do you think?

From original designs by Akiyoshi Kitaoka

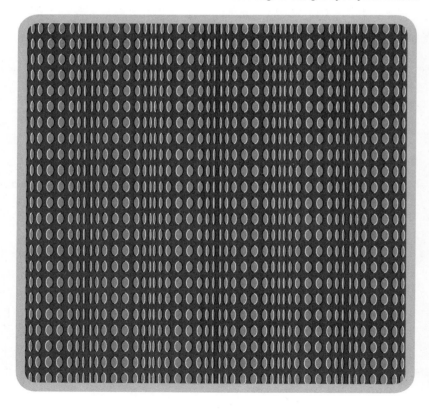

Moving Leaves Illusion

Something is rustling under this pile of leaflike objects. Keep your eyes moving to see illusory motion over the entire image.

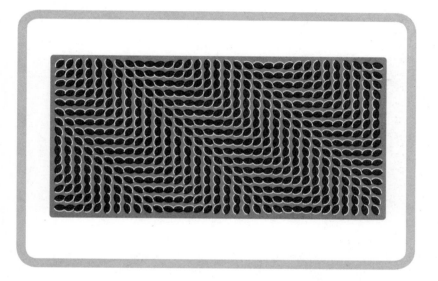

Rotating Doughnut

Keep your eyes moving to see the rotating effect of this contrasting circle design.

From original designs by Akiyoshi Kitaoka

Here is another rotating effect.

From original designs by Akiyoshi Kitaoka

Rotating Trapezoid 1

To see rotating motion in this illusion, hold the image at arm's length with both hands and then move it closer to your eyes as you look at it. Continue the illusory movement by moving the image slowly away again.

Illustration by Arthur Azevedo

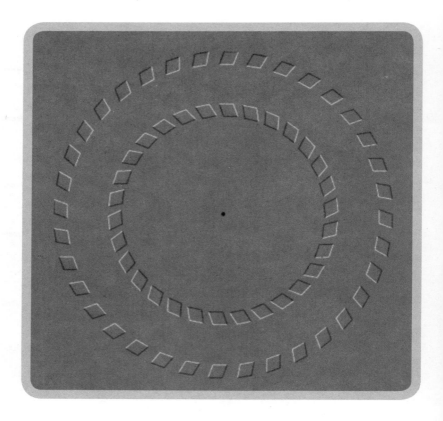

To see rotating motion in this illusion, hold the image at arm's length with both hands and then move it closer to your eyes as you look at it. Continue the illusory movement by moving the image slowly away again.

Illustration by Arthur Azevedo

Rotating Trapezoid 3

To see rotating motion in this illusion, hold the image at arm's length with both hands and then move it closer to your eyes as you look at it. Continue the illusory movement by moving the image slowly away again.

Illustration by Arthur Azevedo

Rotating Trapezoid 4

To see rotating motion in this illusion, hold the image at arm's length with both hands and then move it closer to your eyes as you look at it. Continue the illusory movement by moving the image slowly away again.

Illustration by Arthur Azevedo

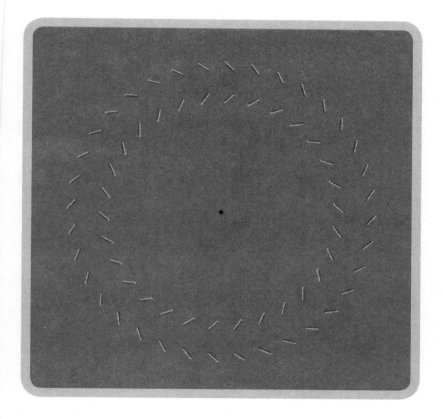

Tsunami Hazard Sign: This international hazard sign for tsunami was recently approved. We can all see the wave, yet part of it is a subjective illusion.

This geometric shape is actually a distorted star with 100 points. The geometry causes a contrast illusion in the bright ring, where the spokes are narrow. The bright white color in the ring is the same as the white color anywhere else. It just looks brighter!

Cast Shadow

In this subjective phrase, the words CAST SHADOW do not exist. The illusion is merely empty space shaped like the words. If you remove the drop shadow, the words will disappear.

These funny looking signs are hiding a secret word, which is also a subjective illusion. Can you solve the puzzle? Remember to see what isn't there!

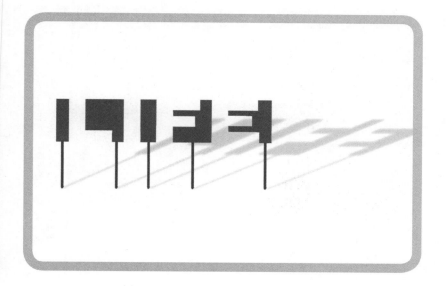

Floating Triangle

The three Pacman shapes help nurture the idea that a solid pyramid is floating between them. The far walls and corner are colluding to create the illusion.

Three Pacman shapes define a three-pointed star illusion in this Kanisaw Illusion. So real is the illusory star that we can easily imagine the curve of the points within the empty spaces.

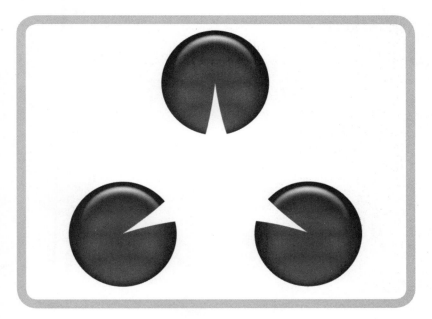

Find the subjective lightbulb in this subjective hidden picture.

These eight gel buttons are fixing some of the features of the famous Necker Cube. Can you visualize the entire wire-framed cube?

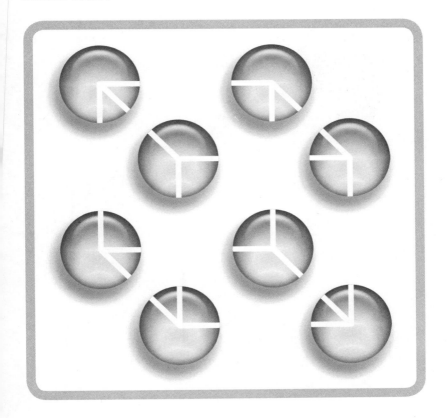

Six-point Star

Three Pacman shapes define a subjective triangle, which, in turn, helps to define a six-point star design.

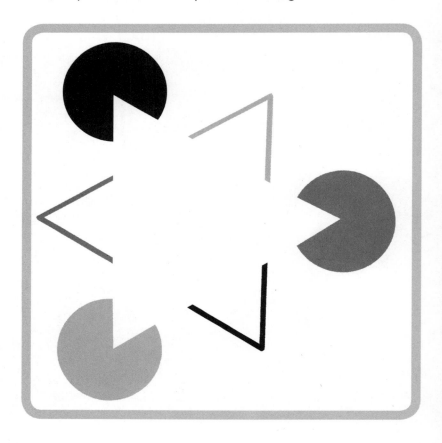

In this design the circle shape is subjective and is defined by line segments, which are painted white. We can also see that the subjective circle is lighter in color and has definite borders inside and out. This is an illusion; there are no borders or a lighter color.

Can you find a wineglass in this hodgepodge of miscellaneous shapes?

Endless Faces Sculpture

A fascinating and easy anamorphic puzzle to solve, no matter how you look at it you always see another face! This image is also special because it is made entirely of keyboard characters. To see this anamorphic changeling clearly, stand off a bit and look at it.

Laura's Eyes Illusion

Here is an example of a relatively new art form known as ASCII Art. The art form is named for the American Standard Code for Information Interchange, an encoding scheme used for computer text characters. The picture is made entirely of keyboard characters. To view this anamorphic illusion, stand back away and look at it. When you see it clearly, Laura's eyes may appear both open and closed.

The Impossible Object and Maze Illusion. Follow the maze through an impossible triangle.

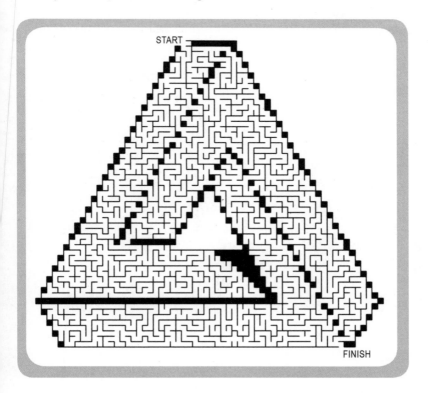

START

FINISH

Ballerina Maze

In the Ballerina Maze and distortion illusion, the two ballerinas are identical and level, yet the dancer on the right appears loftier and somehow different. The illusion is accomplished by simply dropping one of the drop shadows down a bit. Follow the maze from one ballerina to the other.

START

FINISH

See the answer on page 252.

The Mind Reader game will divine your thoughts. Start by checking out the current hand of six cards shown here. Pick one of the cards and memorize it; so this book can get a clear mental reading from you. Ready? Now turn the page...

Carefully scan the hand again, shown here. Is your card missing? Is this the world's first mind-reading book, or a devious trick?

Answer: The second hand is completely different from the first. This book will read your mind no matter which card you choose from the first hand.

Ten Cats Illusion And Maze

In the Ten Cats Illusion and Maze, first find all ten cats in the illustration, then enjoy a romp through the maze.

Find Ten Cats Maze

START

FINISH

See the answer on page 252.

Missing Monk Double Maze

A visiting monk has misplaced his twin brother. Help find the missing twin, and then solve a double dose of mazes.

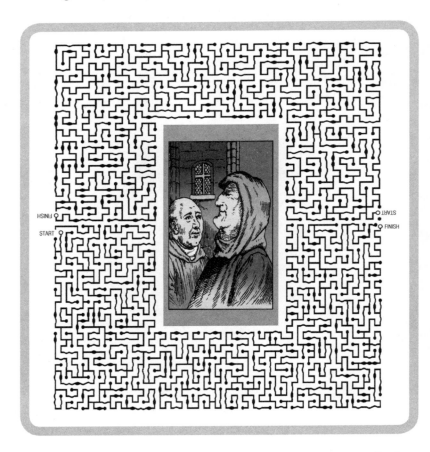

See the maze answer on page 252. Turn the image upside down to find the missing twin—a larger version is available on page 126.

Optical Illusion Wordsearch

Find the words in the puzzle list within the matrix of letters.
Words can be found oriented horizontally, vertically,
diagonally, or backward.

```
J  W  Q  T  L  R  Y  N  E  Y  D  E  W  C  G  O
W  S  U  O  U  G  I  B  M  A  R  T  P  T  W  T
E  V  I  T  I  U  T  N  I  R  E  T  N  U  O  C
H  L  E  L  B  A  T  S  N  U  V  Z  W  I  O  E
L  X  E  G  S  S  E  L  D  N  E  Z  I  M  X  F
J  V  P  P  A  V  R  B  R  Y  R  Z  P  P  D  F
C  R  E  N  J  M  B  X  E  Q  S  L  X  O  F  E
O  C  W  C  P  H  I  T  A  U  I  W  D  S  K  R
T  Y  D  M  A  H  S  R  D  M  B  F  H  S  L  E
E  A  J  W  A  A  A  K  E  P  L  I  Q  I  U  T
B  L  Z  U  R  A  M  N  R  T  E  E  E  B  R  F
J  B  B  T  M  Z  T  O  T  J  F  G  W  L  Z  A
W  G  N  I  G  A  L  F  U  O  M  A  C  E  M  I
N  O  I  T  R  O  T  S  I  D  M  R  P  H  U  X
C  L  A  Y  C  A  J  Z  A  F  J  I  Q  M  A  R
R  T  K  I  N  V  N  O  I  T  O  M  I  F  F  B
```

AFTEREFFECT	COMPLIMENTARY	MINDREADER
AFTERIMAGE	CONTRAST	MIRAGE
AMBIGUOUS	COUNTERINTUITIVE	MOTION
ASPECT	DISTORTION	PHANTOM
CAMOUFLAGING	ENDLESS	REVERSIBLE
COLOR	IMPOSSIBLE	UNSTABLE

See the answer on page 253.

Lincoln's Hat Illusion Maze

Even as a maze, the Lincoln's hat illusion works! The hat is exactly as tall as its brim is wide. Check with a ruler and then solve the maze.

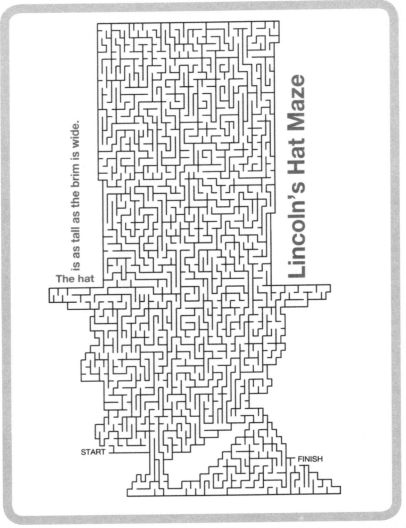

See the answer on page 253.

Become an illusion artist and draw your own optical illusion.
Follow the directions to complete this puzzle.

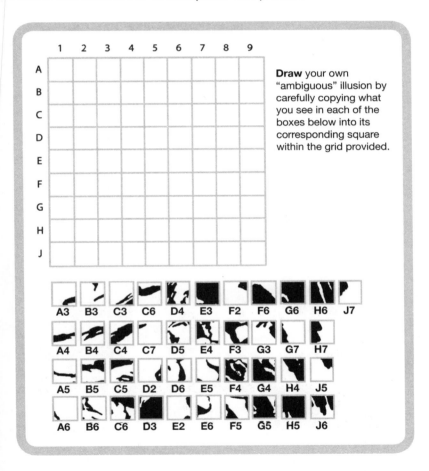

Draw your own "ambiguous" illusion by carefully copying what you see in each of the boxes below into its corresponding square within the grid provided.

Skill-usion 2

Become an illusion artist and draw your own optical illusion. Follow the directions to complete this puzzle.

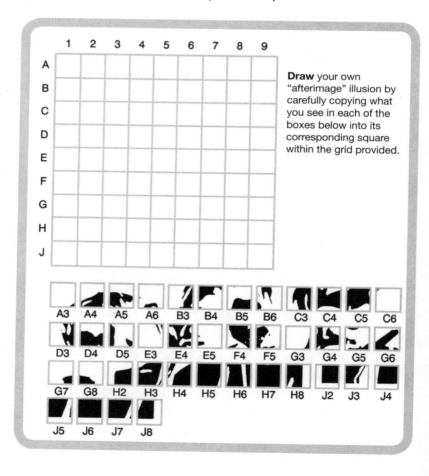

Draw your own "afterimage" illusion by carefully copying what you see in each of the boxes below into its corresponding square within the grid provided.

Become an illusion artist and draw your own optical illusion.
Follow the directions to complete this puzzle.

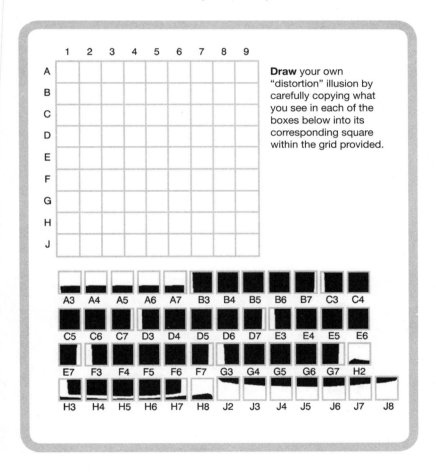

Draw your own "distortion" illusion by carefully copying what you see in each of the boxes below into its corresponding square within the grid provided.

Skill-usion 4

Become an illusion artist and draw your own optical illusion. Follow the directions to complete this puzzle.

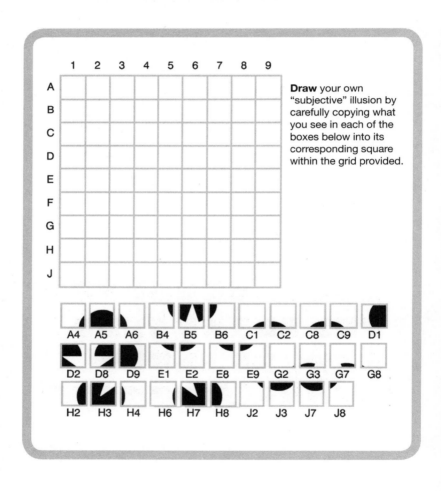

Draw your own "subjective" illusion by carefully copying what you see in each of the boxes below into its corresponding square within the grid provided.

See the answer on page 254.

Become an illusion artist and draw your own optical illusion.
Follow the directions to complete this puzzle.

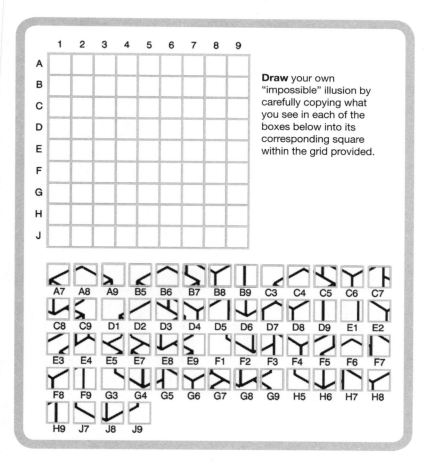

Draw your own "impossible" illusion by carefully copying what you see in each of the boxes below into its corresponding square within the grid provided.

Yin-Yang Mouse Maze

This Yin-Yang Mouse Maze is the ultimate symbol of what the universe stands for, right—wrong, black—white, good—evil, or cheese—pepperoni. If you also see a mouse, you are well on the path to happiness. Work your way through the maze from start to finish.

START

FINISH

See the answer on page 255.

Here is a maze in the Yin-Yang Tao symbol. Have fun!

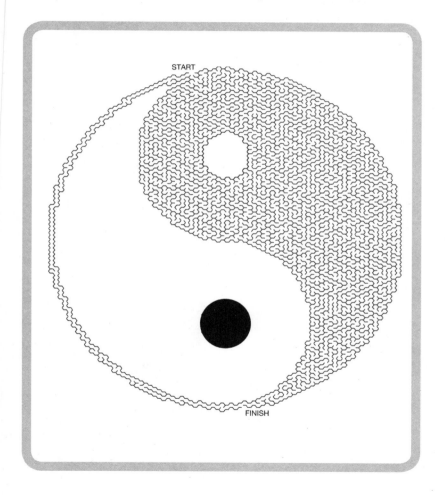

START

FINISH

Solutions

Page 237

Page 238

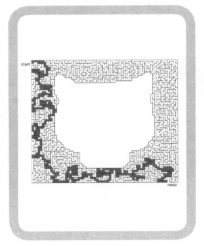

Page 241

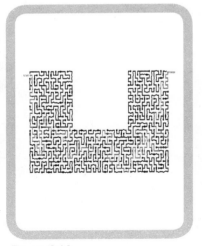

Page 242

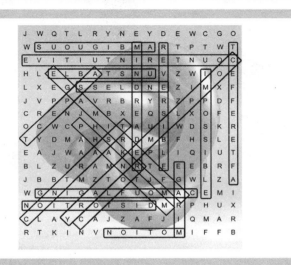

Page 243

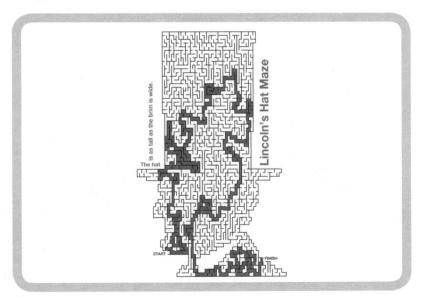

Page 244

Solutions

Page 245

Page 246

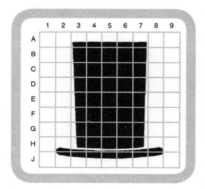

Page 247

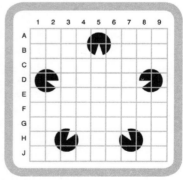

Page 248

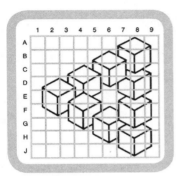

Page 249

Page 250

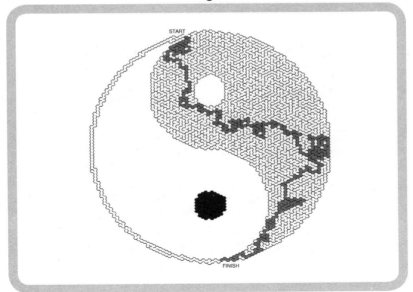

Page 251

Photo Credits